THE BEST OF THE
SALTY CEE

VOL 1

Other books by John Spencer

Not the Bible Titles

Not the Parables of Jesus

More Not the Parables of Jesus

Still More Not the Parables of Jesus

Not the Parable of the Good Samaritan

Not the Christmas Story Vol 1 (with devotional)

Christian Parody Titles

Not the Love Dare

Other books by Nick Angelis

Christian Skits & Such

Nonsense

The Twerk Vaccine

THE BEST OF THE SALTY CEE

VOL 1

CHRISTIAN NEWS SATIRE

John Spencer
& The Salty Cee team

The Best of the Salty Cee Volume 1

Copyright © 2019 John Spencer & The Salty Cee team.

All rights reserved. No part of this book may be copied or reprinted for commercial gain. However, you are more than welcome to share the original articles on social media by linking to our website **www.saltycee.com** . This honours the effort that went into writing them. For other uses please obtain written permission.

The transformation of all spelling into the Queen's English is a subtle power-grab by the British editor over the writers from a certain rebellious colony.

The contents of this book are satire. Satire is using humour to make a point. Though sometimes the point is just to be funny, but it's never meant to be mean. I know this should be obvious from the title, but someone's bound to miss that and get upset. Though if they missed it on the front they're unlikely to notice this warning in the small print. In fact, the only people reading this are likely to be those who read even the terms and conditions of everything. In which case, they know everything except the fact that I am subtly wasting their time by writing nothing in particular. And still they keep reading. When will they learn? It's like they have to obsessively read it all even if it's not important.

Published by:

Kingdom Collective Publishing

Unit 10936, PO Box 6945
London, W1A 6US
kingdomcollectivepublishing@gmail.com

Book cover idea by John Spencer, design by 100covers
The Salty Cee Bible icon – created by Dalmatirac Design Studio
Editing by Katherine.
ISBN: 978-1-912045-91-4

First Edition: June 2019

Dedication

This one's for the fans that have been with us since the beginning.

The Salty Cee team would like to thank both of you.

Your lack of discernment kept us going when we really should have given up.

CONTENTS

SEVENTH DAY ADVENTIST CHICK-FIL-A FRANCHISE: SUNDAY HOURS OFFERED... 9
K-LOVE EXTENDS PLAYLIST ROTATION TO TEN SONGS.................................. 11
JOEL OSTEEN'S FRESHLY POLISHED TEETH GLOW MISTAKEN FOR SHEKINAH GLORY 13
MOVE OF GOD TURNS OUT TO BE INDIGESTION 17
NEW CHURCH ENCOURAGES VAPING TO MIMIC GLORY CLOUD 20
AMBITIOUS DISCIPLE'S RIGHT HAND CAMPAIGN ENDS AWKWARDLY 22
PREDESTIN-O-SCOPES 24
JETS FANS PRAY, GOD ANSWERS. SORTA... 26
CHILDREN'S PASTOR EXCITED ABOUT NEW SECURITY SYSTEM 28
THAI NAVY SEALS CALLED TO FIND HUSBAND LOST IN IKEA 30
SERMON BUZZWORD BINGO... 32
POPE BESTOWS SAINTHOOD ON STAN LEE 33
FIRST RECORDED CHRISTIAN BUMPER STICKER MIND CHANGE....................... 35
LIT WORSHIP SONGS RESULT IN THIRD DEGREE BURNS.................................. 37
VERSE OF THE DAY 39
APPLE WATCH 4 FEATURES "OUT-OF-DATE" COUNTDOWN TIMER 40
STEVEN FURTICK EXPERIENCES REVIVAL DUE TO MIRACLE OF MODERN MEDICINE 42
GLOBAL GRIEF OVER WAREHOUSE MEGACHURCH FIRE 44
TAKE UP YOUR CROSS... 47
NEW PROBE INTO BARABBAS VOTE RIGGING 48
CONVERSION THERAPY CAUSES LEANING TOWER OF PISA TO GO STRAIGHT!...... 50
CHURCH OF THE SALTY CEE CHURCH BULLETIN.. 52
ROB BELL WHAT IS THE BIBLE? ACTIVITY BOOK RELEASED............................. 54
SCIENTISTS DETERMINE THE TIME NEEDED TO PASS BEFORE SECULAR SONGS ARE OKAY FOR CHRISTIAN USE.. 56
TRUE LOVE AT CHURCH CAMPS TO REALLY MAKE IT THIS YEAR, STUDY FINDS .. 58
OBITUARIES 60
NEW TIME UNIT NAMED AFTER WORSHIP LEADER, CHRIS TOMLIN 62
HAIRBRUSH CENTRE OF LOCAL CIVIL CASE.. 64
LIFEWAY ANNOUNCES NEW LINE OF W.W.J.P BRACELETS 66
CHRISTIAN BOOKSTORE PUZZLED BY DROP IN AMY GRANT CASSETTE TAPE SALES 68

LONG-AWAITED BENNY HINN SELF DEFENCE COURSE NOW AVAILABLE FOR PURCHASE 71
MT. CARMEL SHOWDOWN FOR TOWN'S CHURCH HOPPERS 73
CROSSWORD 75
NEW RANGE OF BIBLICAL CLOTHING LAUNCHED 77
ST PAUL'S GARDENING ACCIDENT LEADS TO THORN IN THE FLESH 79
CALVINISTS CELEBRATE DEPRAVITY ON FATHER'S DAY 81
CROSSWORD & JESUKO 83
GDPR COMPLIANCE: GOD DELETES ALL RECORDS OF SIN 85
LADIES BIBLE STUDY BREAKS OUT INTO ACTUAL BIBLE STUDY 87
THANOS OR RAPTURE? CHURCH UNSURE 88
GALILEE 90
HOLY SPIRIT'S BLESSING BLOCKED BY WORSHIP LEADER 91
BIBLE APP ADDS TOOLS TO LIMIT TIME USERS SPEND ON APP 93
THE CAMEL AND THE NEEDLE 95
DAVID PLATT TO STOP TRYING TO CONVINCE CHRISTIANS TO LIVE BIBLICAL LIVES 96
CHURCH DIVIDED OVER PUMPKIN SPICE COMMUNION 98
~~GOSSIP~~ PRAYER REQUESTS AND PRAISES 100
NEW TEST DETERMINES ACCURACY & RELEVANCY OF SCRIPTURES 102
PASTORS BLESS PLANNED PARENTHOOD FOR SUPPORTING PSALM 137 104
PUREFLIX POPULAR CHRISTIAN MOVIE GUIDE CONTAINS PRINTING ERROR..... 106
PERSONAL ADS 108
FIRST BLACK HOLE IMAGE LOOKS LIKE "BLANK SCREEN" 109
STANFORD UNIVERSITY INTRODUCES VBS VOLUNTEER TRAUMA THERAPY PROGRAM 111
TOBY MAC WINS DOVE AWARD FOR MOST THEOLOGICALLY ACCURATE SONG OF THE YEAR 113
PASTOR APPRECIATION MONTH 115
GET THE CEE DELIVERED STRAIGHT TO YOUR SPAM FOLDER! 117
THINK YOU CAN DO BETTER? 118
FEEDBACK 119
ABOUT THE SALTY CEE TEAM 120
OTHER BOOKS BY THE SALTY CEE TEAM 124

FOOD & DRINK

Seventh Day Adventist Chick-Fil-A Franchise: Sunday Hours Offered

For those who have ever wished (the ungodly thought) that Chick-Fil-A was open on a Sunday, there is good news for you! (If you ignore the judgemental attitudes, you'll get from other godlier Christians around you).

In a historic business acquisition earlier this week, a local Chick-Fil-A franchise has changed ownership to a Seventh Day Adventist, Ellen Whitehead.

Ellen Whitehead's spokesperson said that Ellen had always dreamed of owning a fast-food chain but was overwhelmed by the amount of energy and investment involved in making a prophet, I mean profit. When her husband agreed to help her make a go of this amazing opportunity, Ellen signed the papers and the transaction was completed.

Unlike every other Chick-Fil-A in the world, this one will have Sunday hours, but there is a catch: this location will be closed on Saturdays in order to observe the Sabbath.

The other downfall is that Whitehead and her followers do not consume meats, so they won't be able to patronize this restaurant.

But there is good news for those of us who do not hold to Old Testament regulations! We will be able to enjoy the official chicken of Jesus every Sunday after church!

Just when you thought the world was falling apart, light pierced the darkness giving hope to chicken lovers; but alas not at all locations—just this one.

Reporter: **Angry Nursery Worker**

ARTS & MEDIA

K-Love Extends Playlist Rotation to Ten Songs

In a surprise announcement Thursday, K-Love CEO Mike Novak confirmed rumours that the Christian radio station will expand its rotation from the current eight to a whopping TEN songs.

"This is a new frontier for Christian music", said Novak in the statement. "We want to be positive and we want to be encouraging. Now we can do it times ten!"

Stay-at-home mother of six, Megan Jones, doesn't share Novak's excitement. "Do you know how important routine is around here?" she asks as she flips a grilled cheese sandwich with a baby on her hip. "What if there's something we've never heard before? It's ridiculous...it's just a gateway to anarchy!" Megan's seven-year-old Jansen, agrees.

"We like to play 'How many times will Overcomer by Mandisa come on before Daddy cries'. It's usually three. I'll be sad if we only hear it two times now."

Like potlucks and side-hugs, Christian radio is a staple of

Christian culture in America. This makes it dangerous ground to tread on, and K-Love knows it. "Time will tell if this advanced technology will improve the positive, encouraging, K-Love experience for our listeners", conceded Novak. "But I'm convinced and excited for this next big step. Let's see those yahoo's over at Air1 match this!"

Reporter: **Furious Christian**

CELEBRITY NEWS

Joel Osteen's Freshly Polished Teeth Glow Mistaken for Shekinah Glory

Thousands of attendees at Lakewood Church in Houston, Texas this Sunday were led to believe they had received The Favour after the glow from Pastor Joel Osteen's freshly polished teeth was mistaken for the Shekinah glory of God.

"It was a miracle of God! There's no other explanation," exclaimed Vi Moore who said she was sitting with her family in the 6th row.

Added her husband, Shaw Moore, "The Favour of the Lord was upon us! A beautiful light emanated from the stage and bathed us in its warm, welcoming, loving glow." Even their teenage daughter, Ariel Moore, could tell something was different this Sunday. "It was kind of cool, I guess."

Other members in attendance reported experiencing a similar phenomenon. Ren McCormack said that as soon as Pastor

Osteen strode to the middle of the stage, he smiled and a blinding white light shone forth. "I really couldn't see too much, but I felt this inner peace, like the weight of the world, had been lifted from my shoulders. I finally know what Joel means when he talks of The Favour. Words can't describe it, but I know I've been blessed beyond measure."

When asked for a comment, church spokesman Willard Hewitt issued this statement: "Earlier today, many members of our congregation reported a bright light or glow shining from the stage during Pastor Osteen's message. Upon further investigation, including eyewitness accounts, reviewing video feeds from all angles and Pastor Osteen's own testimony, we have concluded that the 'glow' from the stage was the result of the klieg lights reflecting off of Joel's freshly polished teeth. While he has a standing appointment with his dentist, Chuck Cranston, to polish his teeth every Saturday afternoon, Joel was unable to keep yesterday's appointment due to a scheduling conflict. Consequently, his teeth polishing took place just before he walked on stage, resulting in an abnormally bright reflection of the aforementioned klieg lights."

Mr. Hewitt said that, in the future, all teeth whitening and polishing would occur at least 12 hours in advance of Sunday morning services to avoid a similar situation.

Reporter: **Jeff the Comma Head**

ADVERTISEMENT

Christolax

With Christ, all things are possible and he shall make a way where there is no way. He will move that, ahem, mountain for you if you just have faith suppositories.

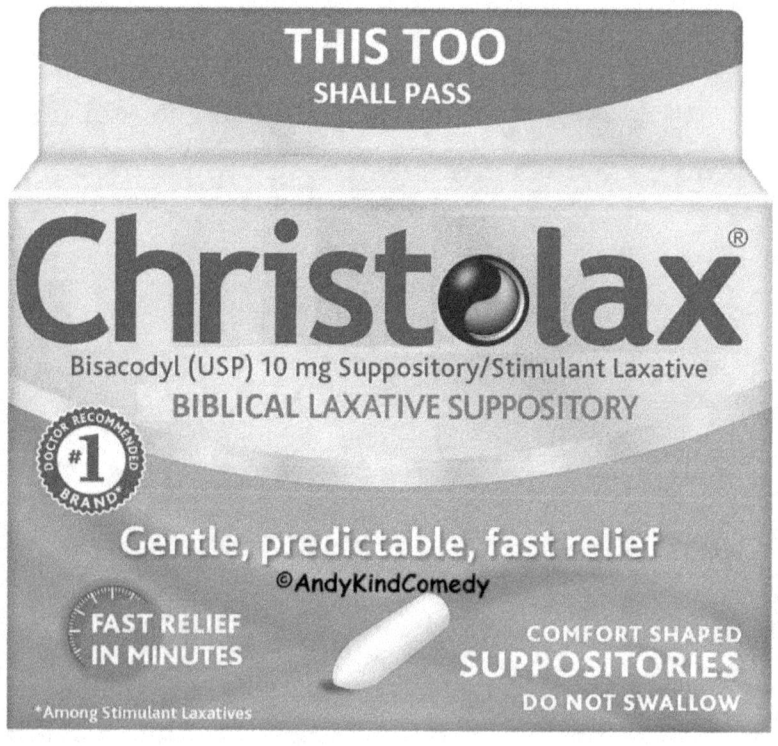

CHURCH NEWS

Move of God turns out to be Indigestion

Pastor Smith of Sturgeon Pentecostal Church, Sturgeon Kentucky had a feeling that Sunday was going to be a good one during the worship as he felt a stirring of the Spirit in his heart.

He leapt to the podium and encouraged his flock with the words, "Don't just sit there! God is here amongst us! I can feel Him! He's here in power and God is mighty and ready to speak to His people."

The congregation went wild as the worship band sang their hearts out with the catchy "Nothing but the blood of Jesus."

By the time Pastor Smith came to preach the Spirit was heavy indeed. He began his sermon with the words, "I feel a weighty presence pressing down on me."

However, that weighty presence overcame the pastor who had to be carried off the platform to the jubilant sounds of the congregation shouting, "Hallelujah!"

The presence remained heavy on the pastor the rest of the day.

So much so that he was unable to eat.

"I feel the LORD calling me to fast during this time!" He declared to his patient wife whilst clutching at his chest.

"Are you feeling okay?" she enquired. "Yes, yes!" He replied.

She remained unconvinced.

After a day of fasting, the presence had only increased. Pastor Smith reported feeling both tense and agitated. He phoned around his flock, instructing them to join him in his time of prayer and fasting as the Spirit was warning him. They must intercede for their community as a time of judgement coming.

A special prayer meeting was called in the church sanctuary. The church faithfully cried out with much travail upon the name of the Lord to save their little town. After four hours, Pastor Smith's wife suggested that a break for some cool iced water would be a good idea.

The pastor thanked his thoughtful wife who could see that he had been deep in travail. He was bent over double, feeling the Spirit's heartache over the manifold sins of their town.

Kindly she offered him some "vitamin tablets" (aka PepcidAC) to take with his water to "keep his strength up" as he continued to press into the Lord in prayer.

Within ten minutes of returning to prayer, he said to his congregation, "My fellow saints! I feel the weight of the LORD has lifted. Our faithful prayers have been heard and judgement has been averted from our beloved town."

When the pastor returned home with his beloved wife, he thanked her once again, extolling her faithful servant heart during those days of trial from the LORD.

She smiled, silently thanking God that He gave at least one of them the gift of discernment.

Reporter: **John Spencer**

CHURCH NEWS

New Church Encourages Vaping to Mimic Glory Cloud

A start up church in Hoboken, New Jersey is encouraging its members and visitors to vape during its Sunday worship service.

Pastor John B. Goode of Revolving Door Fellowship says this practice isn't necessarily to attract hipsters to its fledgling congregation, but it will likely appeal to many in that camp. "It's really only a temporary thing," Goode explained.

"Being a new church, our funds are limited. We really want to get a state of the art fog machine to simulate the glory of God in our services, preferably one with changing colours and strobe features. Rather than buy a budget model, we decided to wait until we can afford a really nice one. After all, nothing is too good for our God."

For added effect, Revolving Door will be providing frankincense and myrrh e-juice to its vapers. "We want it to be as biblical as possible," said Goode.

There are a few glitches that need to be worked out. The first Sunday that vaping was initiated, the smoke was so thick that one visitor was so caught up in the worship that he wandered out the door and over to First Baptist Church without realizing where he was. He said he'd be more careful next time.

Reporter: **Dr Parson Peeves**

BIBLICAL NEWS

Ambitious Disciple's Right Hand Campaign Ends Awkwardly

The Gospels report a strange story about James and John having their mommy ask Jesus for preferential treatment in heaven.

Across all cultures, Mom going to bat for her sons past the age of eight is grounds for removing a corner from their man card or parchment.

It's unclear if other disciples had their third cousins, favourite uncle, least bratty niece, or second best acquaintance who was not a Pharisee ask for similar favours.

The recently discovered Q document, source material for Matthew through Luke, includes an algorithm for places of honour Jesus presumably wrote in the sand several days after that interaction between the Saviour and the Helicopter Parent.

The coveted sit-at-my-right-hand position remains TBA, but the twelve disciples neatly filled other available slots.

While Bartholomew received stand-sheepishly-behind-my-left-shoulder, James was relegated to slouch-in-a-corner-using-your-cell-phone-to-overcome-crippling-social-anxiety.

According to translators, it seems that Jesus appointed John to occasional footstool status.

Reporter: **Dripping Ether**

CALVINIST CORNER

Predestin-o-scopes

Calvinists, find out God's predestined will for you today!

ARIES
You'll meet a tall dark coffee in a shop tomorrow.

TAURUS
Your beard will become a nesting place for birds of all kinds.

GEMINI
The answer you've been waiting for is still 42. Now enough of the procrastination.

CANCER
Remember you said you'd do anything for me except that? Well about that...

LEO
Never forget that you are chosen and saved regardless of what you will do. Except for you Bob, what you're going to do tomorrow is just going to damn you straight to hell. Sorry about that.

VIRGO

You heard the pastor say they needed more help in the nursery.

LIBRA

Yes, that was the Holy Spirit who has been trying to get your attention for the past week and not just toothache.

SCORPIO

Remember that promise you made to me during that emotional worship time. I do.

SAGITTARIUS

That person you've been praying about dating is going to marry some loser. Don't stop praying as it'll help you cope with a life of being single until you die.

CAPRICORN

Confused? That's because you're looking at the wrong promises in the Bible. Try Malachi 2:3.

AQUARIUS

Buying that PlayStation is not my will for you & you know it.

PISCES

That rash is my judgement on you. Stop putting cream on it or I'll send something worse.

SPORTS

Jets Fans Pray, God Answers. Sorta

Florham Park, New Jersey – A small group of New York Jets fans gather to pray every morning at First United Methodist, even though several of the group are of different denominations.

Ronald Andrews, a lifelong fan of the Green and White, broke it down like this for us, "Well, we come from all shapes, sizes, ages, and even denominations. The one thing that really unifies us is our love of the J-E-T-S! JETS! JETS! JETS!!!"

Jerry Phillips, also a Jets fan, stated that their love of football goes even deeper than their love of Christ. "See, in football season, most of us have a deal with the Lord, see. We go to church for the rest of the year, and He understands football season is our time to gather together, encourage one another, you know, build each other up!"

Ronald Andrews agrees, "Jerry, he's a Catholic. Barbara, over there is a Methodist, and well, I'm a Seventh-Day Adventist, so I guess Sunday football games don't really bother me none."

But the real story here comes from the group's recent supernatural experience. "We were prayin' over in the fellowship hall, see," states Jerry, "and we were all askin' the Lord to be with our new QB, Sam Darnold, and to just make sure Teddy Bridgewater's knees hold together, and that Josh McCown can find the right receiver at the right time – bless his heart – and that's when we heard the Lord speak!"

Barbara Wilson, the aforementioned Methodist, believes the Lord spoke clearly, "It was like this, we were praying and seeking the Lord about our Quarterback situation when we heard a still small voice whisper, 'You guys are going to suck again this year.'"

"We knew right then and there," Jerry Phillips stated, "It was gonna be another 16 games of the same old Jets."

Brett Taylor, the youth pastor at First United Methodist and a devout New England Patriots fan was not available for comment. However, security footage from the 7-Eleven across the street saw him scurrying from the building at the precise time the prayer meeting was taking place.

Reporter: **Crass Christian**

CHURCH NEWS

Children's Pastor Excited About New Security System

PACIFICA, CA. As the new year of Sunday school begins at Pacifica Community Assembly, the ultra-hip congregation in the suburbs of San Francisco, Children's Pastor Luke Wade proclaims the preschool is full of exceptional children.

Wade explains further, "We are so excited to have such a great group of children and I'm so grateful for these parents of these exceptional children. One and all, they let me know just how special these kids are, heightening our awareness of the need to keep them safe."

As parents drop off their children in the classroom, each child is checked into the new security system; a quick trip through the metal detector, then past the K-9 bomb sniffing station. A security guard escorts them to class for one last pat down before they are handed over to two FBI background checked and armed Sunday School teachers.

We asked a parent who happened to be dropping off their

precious poppet if the security was a bit too much. He replied, "I suppose it's for the best given the unsettling times we live in now."

With monitored security cameras in each room, the volunteers are freed up to teach, not having worry about any false accusations.

Pastor Wade did have some regrets about having to wait till next year for the retina scanner. However, he thinks they will be okay until next year's budget is in place.

One parent we interviewed did raise a concern about what she viewed to be a major hole in security. She rightly pointed out, "The play area is in an enclosed courtyard but there is no roof over it. Anyone could easily repel from the adjoining roof and snatch one of our precious children before we even knew what happened."

Pastor Wade smiled and wrote down the suggestion while pointing out the 4 armed security guards stationed at all times on the playground.

Reporter: **Peter James**

LOCAL NEWS

Thai Navy SEALs Called to Find Husband Lost in IKEA

On July 5th, Heather Reed and her husband, Randy, visited the massive store to pick up a few things for their kitchen and den. Upon arrival, Mrs. Reed helped her husband navigate through the furniture, past the area rugs and textiles, around the lighting and home office departments, and to the restaurant where Randy would keep himself occupied with Swedish meatballs, chocolate cake, and coffee.

The Reeds set a time and place to meet after Mrs Reed completed her shopping. Randy hasn't been seen since Heather left him at the café.

"We know he's here trying to find his way out." said assistant store manager Sven Karlsson, "But for the moment, he is lost somewhere in our well organised maze of products."

Karlsson continued, "It is our hope Mr. Reed has met up with all the others who have been reported as missing persons within the store. They could use the support of each other."

Upon receiving word that the Thai Navy SEALs have been

contacted and are on route, Mrs. Reed has found renewed hope that her husband will be eventually be found alive and brought to safety. "If anyone can find him, I know those Thai SEALs can." said a tearful Heather on her way to pick up a few more decorations for an upcoming pool party she'll be hosting.

Reporter: **Dr Parson Peeves**

LIFE HACKS

Sermon Buzzword Bingo

Is your pastor's sermon just a little too long?

Does it contain enough buzzwords to sink a battleship?

Why not make use of the Salty Cee's boring sermon buzzword bingo.

cross	season	unpack that	fellowship together
tension	blood	messy	pouring into
loving on	struggle with	Jesus	broken
hedge of protection	doing life together	a heart for	Father

Complete a row, column, or diagonal to win!

Don't forget to stand up and shout "AMEN!" when you do.

You're welcome.

Reporter: **John Spencer**

CULTURE

Pope Bestows Sainthood on Stan Lee

NEW YORK, NEW YORK: The Daily Bugle and their intrepid photojournalist scooped our story today to reveal that Pope Francis has canonized the late Stan Lee, of Marvel Comics fame.

Usually, the process of declaring sainthood takes decades, but the panel of the Congregation for Cause of Saints acknowledged the speed at which today's events start trending, become viral, and quickly end up forgotten. St. Stan will become the patron saint of superheroes. Nightcrawler for one is head over heels over the news.

A Vatican spokesperson had this to say:

"The abrupt nature of this announcement was to ensure that Facebook likes were still being granted to heartfelt posts about Stan Lee's demise from casual fans who may have seen a Marvel movie or two but never opened a comic book. Of course, sainthood does require eyewitness accounts of miracles. In this case, two have been verified: that Stan Lee wrote issues 1-114 of "The Fantastic Four", and that both cinematic adaptations of those lovable misfits were such disasters."

Previous saints, such as Mother Teresa, demonstrated superpowers such as compassion and empathy. Stan Lee is credited with preventing fornication, due to the posters, action figures, and other signs of nerdom adorning the bedrooms of teenage boys, thus acting as a pre-emptive contraceptive. This is also why the pope was able to skip the beatification step for St. Stan.

Likewise, the creators of My Little Pony and Beanie Babies may also be eligible for sainthood on similar grounds once they die, hopefully at a ripe, old, cameo-filled age like Stan Lee has.

Reporter: **Dripping Ether**

EVANGELISM

First Recorded Christian Bumper Sticker Mind Change

The Salty Cee's 10-year investigation of the effectiveness of Christian Bumper Stickers has found its first documented case of someone changing their mind by reading a sticker.

Martha Jones, who is a member of Old Paths Baptist Church has been placing bumper stickers on her 1987 Plymouth Voyager since she bought it in 1999. She began with a simple, "In Case of Rapture, This Car will be Unmanned." Soon she added "You Think It's Hot Out Here," and the powerful "I'm Christian and I vote." The rest is history.

Martha now has over 121 bumper stickers adorning her car. She wondered if those stickers were making a difference but was pleasantly surprised when a former SMU fan told her that she repented of her anger towards her husband who was a Baylor fan after seeing Martha's "House Divided, SMU/Baylor" sticker on her passenger side window.

"What began as a seed of faith has now begun to bear fruit. If

I can change one person's mind, it is worth it." Martha said.

Martha was so encouraged by her success that she just purchased a KJV 1611 window cling to adhere to her front windshield. The Salty Cee will be following this story and will keep you informed.

Reporter: **Northworst Seminary**

WORSHIP NEWS

Lit Worship Songs Result in Third Degree Burns

What started off as the usual Friday night youth worship event at the Real Agape Warehouse that included some lit worship songs ended up like a scene out of a disaster flick.

"The band and I were rocking some great tunes," explained guitarist Jamie 'Jed' Delacruz, "We were really jamming as we sang 'Wild One' by Sean Feucht with the refrain, 'Set Us on Fire.'"

Bass player, 'The Big D' took up the story were Jed left off as Jed welled up, "It was crazy man, we had only sung it about 267 times when the heavens opened and fire came down."

The drummer, 'Baz', interrupted, "It was like something out of Acts except this was real flames. He paused thoughtfully. "I'm not sure whether the screaming counted as speaking in tongues though."

Vocalist Jenny added, "God was answering our prayers and it was like amazing until we realised that he had taken our cool lyrics literally."

The tragic result of this Mount Carmel experience was that about 70% of the youth sustained third-degree burns at the event. Those who managed to escape relatively unscathed were 'lost in worship' and swayed with their eyes closed until they smelt something burning.

"I thought the evening was going to finish with a hog roast or something," stated Emily, "When I opened my eyes, I realised the noise wasn't coming from people running to get to the front of the line. They were all making a beeline to the baptismal tank."

That mad rush led to the youth pastor to mistake the event for a revival, "I was like, man, God has worked through these lit worship songs and now people are wailing over their sins and getting baptised. Then I saw the fire and called 911."

One thing's for sure, the youth will be more careful about what they sing in the future.

Jed concluded, "Yeah when we sing that song we now say 'Set us on fire metaphorically'"

Reporter: **John Spencer**

DEVOTION

Verse of the Day

"Go, take to yourself a wife of whoredom and have children of whoredom..." -

Hosea 1:2

TECHNOLOGY

Apple Watch 4 Features "Out-of-Date" Countdown Timer

The Apple Watch 4 was announced on September 12 and is available for pre-order right now.

It boasts the same shape and screen display as the previous three models, together with the same specifications and apps as before. However, this exciting upgrade comes with a different coloured strap.

And if that's not enough to make you part with your hard-earned money, it comes with an all-new countdown timer that lets you know when your series 4 Apple watch will be superseded by the next model.

No longer do you need to worry about being out-of-date and missing out on spending more money on exactly the same watch but in a stylish new colour.

This countdown timer lets you know exactly when you'll part with your cash.

Apple COO Jeff Williams stated, "Previously, we used to just slow down the old Apple watch software with an update so that customers would eventually get so annoyed by the slowdown that they'd purchase the latest product. However, extensive testing has shown a klaxon alarm is over 1000% more effective that the excessive update methodology."

Williams continued, "We toyed with the watch announcing 'unclean' to let people know how unhip they were by still using an old series watch, but the alarm reflects how we and our shareholders feel about people who don't buy our latest model."

The Apple watch 4 also received clearance from the U.S. Food and Drug Administration (FDA) to be a safe way of eating money.

"Apple is now empowered to take more control of their buyers' bank accounts," said FDA Commissioner Scott Gottlieb in a statement.

The Apple Series 4 watch is available for ONLY $9,999 with a discount offered in exchange for any family members sold into slavery.

Reporter: **John Spencer**

CELEBRITY NEWS

Steven Furtick Experiences Revival Due to Miracle of Modern Medicine

Sources confirmed today that Steven Furtick suffered a loss of consciousness during a staff meeting at Elevation Church, earlier this week.

"He was sweating and slurring his words and he seemed to be short of breath when all of a sudden. His eyes rolled back in his head and he crumpled to the floor," said one Elder Board member who was present at the meeting but wished to remain anonymous. "We immediately called 911 and laid him out on the table."

The first responders on the scene immediately observed that Pastor Furtick's super skinny jeans were cutting off blood flow to his brain. "He regained consciousness within moments after we cut off his jeans as the blood could then flow freely," said EMT Joshua Pardo. "When you've been on the job as long as I have, you learn to spot this sort of thing right away. That's why we always carry a pair or two of spare sweatpants."

Multiple elders of Elevation have reported that since switching to those loose-fitting pants, Pastor Furtick's theology has become transformed.

"Why, just yesterday, I saw him in his office with a Bible open in front of him and a stack of reference books with a copy of Strong's Exhaustive Concordance right on top...and he was reading them!" said Pastor Furtick's personal secretary. "Apparently, those tight fitting skinny jeans he always wore was cutting off blood flow so much that it affected his mental faculties, causing him to make wild and crazy pronouncements from the pulpit."

Reporter: **Jeff the Comma Head**

CHURCH NEWS

Global Grief over Warehouse Megachurch Fire

Only days after the Notre Dame Cathedral fire brought international responses with help, another church fire has brought a global outpouring of grief.

This time it was at the Grace Synergy megachurch main campus, a seemingly nondescript, big box, multi-purpose facility in Wichita, Kansas built from a converted warehouse.

The fire started during the Friday worship experience and led to over 200 young people being treated for smoke inhalation at the local hospital.

"At first we thought we must have left the fog machine on," said Jaxon Phillips, the worship leader, "or maybe the vaping had got out of hand. But as people were falling on the ground the tenth time through the bridge, I realised that either this was the glory cloud or the building was on fire. I took no chances, grabbed my luxury sneakers and ran for the exit."

Flames soon engulfed the building and while fireman sought

to bring the fire under control the town's residents gathered around weeping and singing Oceans.

Except for the bassist who just stood and swayed as there was nowhere to plug in.

There was a palpable sense of reverence amongst the people over the loss of this sacred space.

Megachurch pastor Steve Starr added, "We followed our emergency action plan and managed to save the Van Der Westen Speedster coffee machine and a small number of flags used by our prophetic dance group."

The fire was put out in the early hours of the morning, leaving the building a shell of its former shell. But long before then the international community had expressed its solidarity with Pastor Steve and over three billion dollars had been pledged to help rebuild this cultural icon bigger and better than before.

"It was a blessing in disguise. We knew our online campus was growing, but this really set it ablaze" said the Jed "The Man" Manson, Director of Online Vibes, "I think it was the functional utility of the building that captured the imagination of millions around the globe."

The leadership team are already drawing up plans for a state-of-the-art multimedia auditorium with a coffee shop, vaping bar and mini-golf course.

The cause of the fire is as yet unknown, but already fingers are pointing at members of Westboro who were picketing outside yelling and holding signs: "God is impartial" and "Judgement on the heretics".

If you were moved by the loss of this holy venue and would like to donate then please click here.

Idea by **Drew Dyck** with additional reporting by **Marshall Gallagher, Hipster Evangelical, Derek Hiebert, Pastor Scott, Mark Brown** and **John Spencer.**

CARTOON

Take up your cross

Dang it, Peter. I said "take up YOUR CROSS".

@Furious_Xtian

BIBLICAL NEWS

New Probe into Barabbas Vote Rigging

New evidence has been unearthed that throws doubt on the legitimacy of Barabbas' release on the Passover feast in 30 AD.

The Israeli Antiquities Authority recently unearthed a primitive polling machine used by the Roman governor Pilate in such decisions.

However, closer inspection shows that this machine was set up in such a way to rig the results.

Benjamin Mintz commented, "It is clear that the governor was involved in collusion of the results, but the question remains, 'with whom?'"

He continued, "Traditionally, the finger was pointed at the Pharisees and Sadducees but we also unearthed some Russian coins in the square outside of the praetorium. Given that Rome never conquered that far, these coins must have come here with travellers.

I think it's no coincidence! This clearly shows that there was Russian interference with the voting that led to the release of Barabbas."

Reporter: **John Spencer**

LIFESTYLE

Conversion Therapy Causes Leaning Tower of Pisa to Go Straight!

The Leaning Tower of Pisa is known worldwide for its tilt, today revealed that due to extensive conversion therapy over the last 17 years it is now going straight.

According to therapist professor Nunziante Squeglia, the 57-metre (186ft) building straightened by 4cm (1.5in).

LGBT activists are horrified by the news and have condemned the therapy saying it is dangerous and harmful to tourist attractions worldwide.

However, the professor responded saying, "What counts the most is the stability of the bell tower, which is better than expected."

According to Queer Theory, tourist attractions are constructed straight or bent and they are not influenced by the environment. However, some engineers say that the tilt of buildings is influenced over time by layers of clay and sand underneath.

"In this case, the layer is softer on the south side compared to the north, which meant that even though the building was straight by the time it grew to the third storey the soil had unsettled its foundations. This can be treated over time with love and care."

However, opponents, not convinced, have stated that the Leaning Tower of Pisa is only denying its true identity and have moved to get the Italian government to outlaw the use of such treatments.

Reporter: **John Spencer**

NOTICES

Church of the Salty Cee Church Bulletin

The Church of the Salty Cee Church Bulletin: Keeping you up-to-date, in-the-loop and ear-to-the-ground on all the ~~gossip~~ events that will be happening this week.

UPCOMING EVENTS

Tuesday, 9/25 at 8AM we are having our regularly scheduled prayer meeting. Gladys reassures that her uncle from Kentucky is no longer visiting and Gladys' family apologizes for all the snakes he brought last week.

Saturday, 9/29, 1PM-3PM is our annual Wash & Give. The youth will be taking donations to wash and vacuum your vehicles, along with the church vans. All loose change, French fries, and hard candy collected from the seat creases and floors of the vehicles will be donated to our sister city in Port-au-Prince: Hungry, Hungry, Haitians.

Sunday 10/7 following service Deacon John Spencer will host the newcomer luncheon in the fellowship hall. John will spend a few minutes on the history of the church, arbitrary doctrines, and why the letter 'u' is randomly thrown into British words for no apparent reason.

ANNOUNCEMENTS

Youth Group Movie Night: Big Trouble in Little China cancelled after realizing the Chinese having "lots of hells" is a false doctrine.

Youth Pastor Search: In the interest of time, the Board has met and pre-emptively plans to dismiss the future youth pastor for his poor performance that will show up in six months' time.

The **Marriage Matters** class will resume next week, as Jerry Grynn and Heather Barrett will share their testimonies of hope and triumph in persevering through a third divorce. Tuesdays at 6pm in room 102.

Reporter: **Furious Christian**

ARTS & MEDIA

Rob Bell What is the Bible? Activity Book Released

Successful author Rob Bell has released an activity book to accompany his recent book "What is the Bible?"

It is designed to appeal to liberal Christians everywhere and includes activities such as:

- Colouring – use opaque pens to colour out Biblical passages that don't match your view of God and the afterlife.

- Word search – find the passages that confirm God is all loving and doesn't require anything of us

- Mazes – see if you can get from the start of the Bible to the finish without stumbling across its true meaning

- Dot-to-dot – join up unrelated passages together to give a whole new interpretation

- Logic puzzles – fill in the grid by ignoring the clues and following your feelings on the subject.

Available from all undiscerning bookshops everywhere.

Reporter: **John Spencer**

SCIENCE

Scientists Determine the Time Needed to Pass Before Secular Songs Are Okay for Christian Use

Columbus, OH – 23 years, three months and 4 days.

This is the exact amount of time scientists have determined needs to pass before a secular song can be used in the church for media, skits, interpretive dance, and/or badly sung by the senior pastor during a sermon.

Contrary to previous thought, statisticians proved that any indulgences in secular music before this specific time can cause major issues within different groups in a church.

One notable example was the inclusion of the 1996 hit "Who Will Save Your Soul" by Jewel in a teen skit performed this past May at the First Baptist church.

Chaos ensued as some elderly women fainted and armchair theologians in the congregation started a new forum online regarding the sinful nature of the song. The senior pastor included scathing rebukes in three sermons, referencing the heretical skit, and for four families the skit was the final straw.

One father stated, "We should just go to that new church our cousin keeps talking about".

Oddly enough, the 1995 hit, "Wonderwall" was accidentally played during an altar call at the Second Baptist church, after the media department's Spotify playlist went rogue.

Several people rededicated their lives while others remarked that the altar call was a turn in the right direction for the church.

More research will be conducted regarding the genre of the music.

Reporter: **ProtestANT-Man**

RELATIONSHIPS

True Love at Church Camps to Really Make It This Year, Study Finds

Tulsa, Oklahoma – If you're looking for true love, but you are an introverted, lonely, or just all out unattractive, insecure teenager going to church camp this summer, you're in luck!

A new study released today states that church camp relationships are set to increase by a total of 200% this summer. Dr Erin Gardner, Professor of Adolescent Psychology at North Central Bible Community College and author of "Young Love and Why It Really Will Last This Time," stated that this study "probably, can totally, well, almost be trusted."

Dr Gardner led the study along with several teenagers from local youth groups, who were promised free pizza upon completion of their participation.

Due to a combination of economic growth within the United States, a boom of summer blockbusters in the movie theatre, and the fact that public transportation is more reliable than your mother's Chevy Equinox, a successful romance is almost guaranteed. That is, if you're willing to meet halfway. That young romance you made at your church camp will almost certainly make it to the beginning of the school year this fall.

"The real wild card in this whole process," Dr Gardner claimed, "is whether or not the couple can maintain the relationship through social media well enough to last until August. It also depends on whether or not they're able to balance their budding relationship with school and other extracurricular activities."

Chances are, according to those teenagers who participated in the study, this year is the year that true love really does mean true love. This time.

Reporter: **Crass Christian**

NOTICES

Obituaries

Enoch

Died, aged 365 years. Enoch was the father of Methuselah and other sons and daughters. Last seen walking with God over a year ago and hasn't been seen since. Presumed dead or extremely crafty at playing hide and seek.

Ananias and Sapphira

Died, age unknown. Ananias and Sapphira were property owners and apparently generous members of their fellowship. Having recently sold some land, they donated the full proceeds to the church fund. As a result of their charitable act, the couple was being considered for the role of deacons.

Sadly, both died on the same day. Cause of death is still unknown but may be linked to a recent church pot luck.

Your sense of humour

Died unexpectedly within the last hour. Seemed fine before you started reading this book but quickly developed symptoms of failing soon after. The Salty Cee team strenuously deny responsibility.

It is coincidental that your sense of humour as well as multiple other readers of this book experienced the same thing at the same time.

Honest.

CELEBRITY NEWS

New Time Unit Named After Worship Leader, Chris Tomlin

Chris Tomlin has already won Dove and Grammy awards for his songs, but to have physicists vote to name a new unit of measure after him leaves those trophies in the dust.

It has long been known that eight words of the song "How Great is Our God! (Sing with me)" are repeated for what seems like an eternity. Thus, MIT physicists have dubbed a new time unit "The Tomlin" to describe a situation that feels like an infinity of time.

Relativity theory means that what can feel like an eternity during a worship song is, in actuality, only about 20 minutes. It is this distortion of reality experienced during Chris Tomlin's songs that lead the scientists to use his name to describe this bizarre phenomenon.

"I am honoured to have received this award in recognition of the enduring and endless nature of our God and my songs that reflect this characteristic," Tomlin said in a press release.

It's not the first time the singer has received recognition for this feature of his worship songs, apparently the 80s film "The Never Ending Story" was inspired by Tomlin's first youth worship concert.

It has sadly been reported that the singer has recently been diagnosed with functional limb weakness in both his arms. Doctors believe this is a result of Tomlin holding them up, extended to heaven, for the full duration of his worship hit "I Lift My Hands," averaging anywhere between 25 and 30 minutes at his live concerts.

Reporter: **Angry Nursery Worker**

LEGAL NEWS

Hairbrush Centre of Local Civil Case

COUNTERTOP, USA – Formal charges were filed Monday in civil court over, of all things, a hairbrush.

Famed children's programming actor Lawrence Q. Cumber is suing lifelong friend and business partner Robert DiTomate over the hairbrush, alleging it was stolen and traded off to a local pawn shop, Peach's Pawns.

Close sources say Cumber and DiTomate, once the best of friends, have not spoken to one another in months.

Cumber is seeking five dollars in restitution plus court costs. DiTomate's lawyer, Archibald Sparagus released the following statement:

"Mr. DiTomate is a highly respected member of the community, and does not take these accusations lightly. We are preparing a counter-suit for the slanderous accusations and emotional damage due to Mr. Cumber."

A hearing is scheduled for August to determine if a settlement can be reached.

Reporter: **Furious Christian**

FASHION

Lifeway Announces New Line of W.W.J.P Bracelets

In a bid to capture more of the Millennial Antifa market, Lifeway recently announced a line of What Would Jesus Protest™ bracelets.

"With Millennials facing micro-aggressions, triggers, cis-gendered patriarchy and the existence of people who believe differently than they do," said a Lifeway spokesperson, "It's hard for them to know what, when, or how to protest. I mean, there are so many protests to choose from, sometimes several in one day. This bracelet, hopefully, will prompt them to carefully consider and prioritize their protests according to what Jesus would get triggered by."

In order not to offend anyone, the new bracelets will only be available in a rainbow gradient. However, users can choose from one of 47 different gender styles.

Reporter: **Jeff the Comma Head**

ADVERTISEMENT

Tide Pod Communion Wafers

The blood of Christ cleanses us from every sin.

But sometimes you need that little something extra to remove that stubborn sin that just won't go.

That's why we recommend the all new tide pod communion wafers.

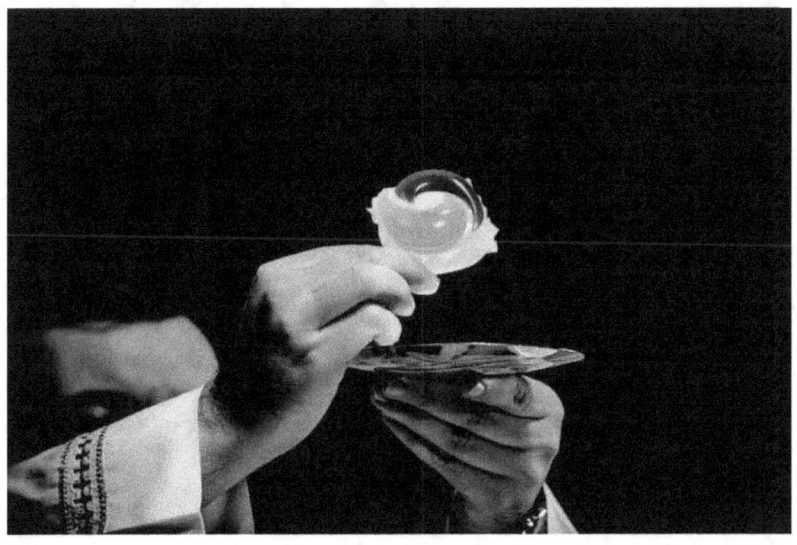

BUSINESS

Christian Bookstore Puzzled by Drop in Amy Grant Cassette Tape Sales

EUREKA SPRINGS, AR–Independent Christian bookstores are similar to that expensive food and vitamin store in your town: no one has the heart to tell the owners that even Wal-Mart has a gluten-free section, or that the last time a customer bought a product from the "New Age Spirituality" aisle, kale chips and promise rings were trending.

And that's just the tip of the iceberg: do they know that TBN's founders Paul and Jan Crouch are dead and that vaccines and whole wheat aren't the bedrock of health and prevention for most of their customers anymore?

To answer these questions, we interviewed Jim Bungarde, the bespectacled owner of the aptly named "Christian Bookstore" located across from the Herb Co-Op.

"I know that we are the only ones who've been in the store all day, but I think we're going to make a profit this year, for the first time since Focus on the Family's 'McGee and Me' videos were flying off the shelves. All of those emptied shelves are now filled with this new book called The Purpose Driven Life. These hip, young, trim pastors—Matt Chandler, Joel Osteen, TD Jakes, John Hagee—are writing inspirational books that my customers love. And the godly ethics of these people! The Jimmy Swaggart and Bakers of this world could learn a few things from the likes of Paula White-as-snow, as I like to call her. "

There was slight pause in the interview as our reporter choked on his green smoothie. But once he recovered, he quickly wiped the traces of cucumber and junior asparagus from the stack of Veggie Tales VHS tapes. The conversation then shifted to the billion-dollar industry of Christian music.

"I don't understand why Amy Grant doesn't resonate with her fellow God-fearing teenagers anymore," Mr. Bungarde continued, as we wiped green smoothie from his glasses.

"Her new album is doing okay, but her cassette tape sales have just really fallen off. Her hair isn't as big on her newer CDs, maybe that's the problem. Or do you think Rebecca St. James is stealing her fans? Her hair is bigger than Amy's, maybe that's it. Bottom line is, eight-tracks of Stryper's 'The Black and Yellow Attack' are still selling briskly.

I think it's just a temporary glitch that the youth aren't coming in here to buy my Amy Grant tapes. Maybe I should put them on sale, next to the promise rings made from dehydrated kale."

Reporter: **Dripping Ether**

CELEBRITY NEWS

Long-Awaited Benny Hinn Self Defence Course Now Available for Purchase

FIJI—After years of successfully slaying people in the Spirit in their thousands, Benny Hinn has finally created the ultimate self-defence course where he shares the secret of his gifting in a really rather nice package.

With the rise of violence and terrorism worldwide, Hinn (age 65 ½) tells our correspondent, who is actually a 12-year-old kid bored on summer vacation, that God spoke to him and told him to multiply his gift of healing and self-defence (for a nominal fee of course) to help fellow brothers and sisters out.

This riveting series will help protect the flock from demons, disease and intruders; as well as stomach aches, bad breath, and acne.

Just look for the clickbait logo and follow the link. The price may be a little too much to pay up front, but our staff believes that a 30-year financing plan at 4% interest should be easy for most people to afford.

Don't miss out on this offer and if you order in the next 10 minutes, you can get a second self-defence kit for the same price!

Available on DVD, Blu-ray, Laserdisc, VHS, MP4 format, and braille hardcover book form.

*Boxing gloves not included.

Reporter: **Angry Nursery Worker**

CHURCH NEWS

Mt. Carmel Showdown for Town's Church Hoppers

Church hoppers are one of a pastor's greatest frustrations. They attend for a while, checking out your church's worship styles, preaching methods, and playground size, but are taken aback when you as their pastor ask them to - horror or all horrors – serve. Maybe they heard another church was cooler or maybe they noticed that sinners attend your church.

Whatever the reason, they move to the next church for a couple of months before repeating the cycle all over again.

Well for the pastors of Springdale, Arkansas the endless church hopping between the twenty churches became too much.

Together they summoned all the Christians in the town to the top of Mount Magazine, the highest peak in Arkansas, and addressed them:

"How long will you waver between our churches? If Agape Fellowship is your church then commit to it, if Temple Baptist church is your church then commit to it..."

"Gather twenty platforms for us. And let each pastor preach repentance from their pulpit. The one who causes you to fall to your knees weeping is the pastor of your church."

Then all the Christians said, "What you say is good."

And so, the pastors each took a turn preaching, each causing a portion of the people gathered to wipe tears from their eyes and confess their manifold sins.

Those people were added to their congregation for good.

All went well until the local liberal pastor spoke. Her sermon on inclusivity made everyone feel like God owed them for their wonderful life choices. So, the evangelical pastors cried out:

"Shout louder! Surely your theology is right! Perhaps it is deep in eisegesis, or busy listening to the world, or traveling to its safe space. Maybe it is sleeping and must be awakened to the true faith."

But sadly, to no avail. Fortunately, the police presence prevented any of these pastors calling on people to seize the liberal pastor and slaughter them in the nearby valley.

Reporter: **John Spencer**

CULTURE

Crossword

This month's crossword is "heck", a mild expression of surprise, frustration, dismay or disgust:

"Oh heck, I did not expect that!"

Can also be used for emphasis in both questions and exclamations:

"What the heck is that?"

"It could have been a heck of a lot better."

Often it is used to express when something is remarkable:

"We had a heck of a good time."

Heck is actually a late 19th Century euphemism for the place where you go if you don't believe in Gosh.

As such it is considered appropriate for most Christians and their children over the age of 5 and can be used to replace that less suitable word wherever it might occur:

- Heck-icopter – a Christian approved flying machine
- Heck-o – a Christian approved greeting to one another

- Heck-enisation – a Christianised version of Greek culture and thought, popularised by Augustine and Thomas Aquinas.

- Heck-pmeet – a man's wife, a word considered much more acceptable by egalitarians

- Heck Boy – a comic and film that is still considered inappropriate even with this euphemism

However, its rather overlooked etymology is less able to be ignored when it is used in a more explicit manner. Clearly inappropriate usage would include:

"What the heck do you care?"

"Get out of my hecking face."

However, most Christians would consider letting these uses slide if used by youth pastors to "engage the culture of the young people".

RUDENESS : 1/5

EXPRESSIVENESS: 1/5

DANGER OF LOSING SALVATION: 1/5
(unless youth worker, in which case 0/5)

FASHION

New Range of Biblical Clothing Launched

LifeWay may have closed their physical bookstores due to the efforts of conservative Christians, but that hasn't stopped them expanding their range online.

After the success of the "What Would Jesus Protest" bracelets for young Millennials, they decided to move into more biblical territory with a range of clothing based on bible verses.

First up is the "As the Deer Pants" based on Psalm 42 and featuring a lovely deer. Different versions have been released for the US and UK markets to overcome the confusion over the translation of pants in the Hebrew.

Conservative Christians have complained that the position of the aforementioned deer could lead to people meditating on things other than the Bible verse.

Robes of Righteous are due for release by Easter. Robes of Self-Righteousness will be available for modern day Pharisees as well as platform shoes for the vertically challenged who still want to look down on others.

Finally, Lifeway has plans to make clothing for those who want to mourn according to the law by tearing their clothes, but who don't actually want to ruin their clothing. This line of shirts features Velcro strips that allow easy removal of the arms and collar, going as far as to expose part of the shoulder to give that authentic impression of deep lamentation.

Reporter: **John Spencer**

BIBLICAL NEWS

St Paul's Gardening Accident Leads to Thorn in the Flesh

Paul was trimming his rose hedge when he experienced a thorn in the flesh - in his index finger to be precise.

It could have happened to anyone and most people would have swiftly pulled it out.

However, Paul realised this so-called accident was because he had become conceited over his superior gardening skills. Thus, the thorn was a messenger of Satan sent to torment him.

And he cried out three times unto the Lord for Him to take it away.

But God did reply, "My grace is sufficient for you, for my power is made perfect in weakness."

So, Paul realised that God was asking him to man up and use tweezers to remove the thorn from his flesh despite the potential endless digging around that always hurts just so much.

Next week, we'll report on how Paul cried out for God to remove sand from his eye.

Reporter: **John Spencer**

CULTURE

Calvinists Celebrate Depravity on Father's Day

What better way for Calvinists to celebrate Father's Day 2018 than to point out the depravity of their earthly fathers.

The children gathered around their father's bed first thing in the morning and recited the manifold failings of their earthly father. Immediately following, each child took a turn to list the mistake their father made that had caused them the most hurt.

"It was a beautiful time," said Jim, father of 4 children, "I love how they all came together as family to tell me of my sins."

"Thinking that I'm an okay dad is a common temptation of mine," says Bruce from Illinois, "but Father's Day is a great reminder of just how much I've messed up my kids. I mean I had no idea just how poor a job I have done that year."

But what do the children make of this?

"Some of my friends at school build up resentments and it eats them up inside," said Josh aged 8, "But there's something so cleansing about just letting my dad know how rubbish he is, how he's let me down, and messed me up psychologically."

"In our family after we peppered our dad with all the things he did wrong, he hit himself with a stick saying 'Mea Culpa'," said little Maisy aged 5.

Reporter: **John Spencer**

PUZZLES

Crossword & Jesuko

This tricky cryptic Christian crossword puzzle will have you guessing for hours.

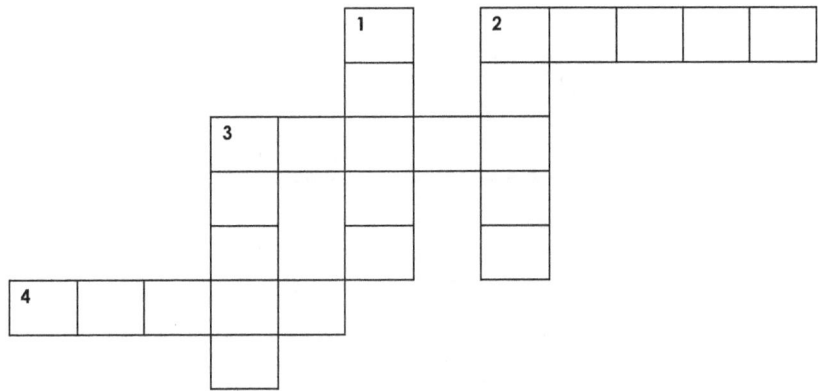

ACROSS

2. Came to seek and save the lost

3. Calmed the storm

4. Sounds like the chord Gsus

DOWN

1. Firstborn over creation

2. Died on a cross for our sin

3. Is the answer to every Sunday School question

Tried Sudoku and long for something more spiritual?

Well, have no fear – we've combined Sudoku and Jesus to make Jesuko. The ultimate in Christian puzzles.

Ensure that every row, column and 2x2 square contain all of the 4 different letters from Jesus' name:

		E	
J			
	U		S

BUSINESS

GDPR Compliance: God Deletes All Records of Sin

The GDPR (General Data Protection Regulation) in the EU requires that anyone who processes data to:

- inform subjects of the specific purpose for which their data is used
- obtain consent from those subjects
- inform them of their right to withdraw consent at any time

Being omnipresent and omniscient means that God naturally collects data from everyone everywhere, including items such as the number of hairs on people's heads. But despite making clear that He will judge the living and the dead – many people seem to be unaware of this.

Attempts by Christians to increase awareness that "God is watching" have not only been rebuffed but, in many cases, outlawed as bigoted hate speech.

However, many of those who have become aware have made use of the provisions of the GDPR to request that God delete all records of their sins, particularly 'Sensitive Personal Data' that they wouldn't want their wives or co-workers to know about.

For Christians, GDPR has made little difference as God "will remember their sins no more" (Jer 31:34).

However, for those who choose to reject Jesus, this law has created a bit of a dilemma for God. How can He rightly condemn people and send them to hell when there is no record of their wrongs?

Satan has also expressed displeasure at the ruling.

However, a spokesperson for Rob Bell was ecstatic, "This law is a victory for progressive Christians everywhere and celebrates the God of love whom we have created in our image."

Reporter: **John Spencer**

CHURCH NEWS

Ladies Bible Study Breaks Out into Actual Bible Study

The Ladies Bible Study at Glory Fellowship have been meeting for 10 years to discuss the events going on in their community and especially within the church. Their discussions usually result in "praying" for the pastor and his family's shortcomings. They also "pray" for those they suspect of having affairs and the members they saw going into the local liquor store.

But this past Tuesday, the women actually ran out of things to "pray" for, so they decided to open the Bible. An amazing thing happened. The women found out that their "Prayer Times" are talked about in the Bible. Under conviction, the women agreed to stop "Praying" and to begin studying the Bible.

Reporter: **Northworst Seminary**

CHURCH NEWS

Thanos or Rapture? Church Unsure

Thanos, who is no stranger for receiving blame for everything and anything that goes wrong, recently issued a statement denying responsibility when YouTube went down.

Whilst we at the Cee wouldn't condone such Thanos blaming, we understand how it has become more prevalent in this day and age. As atheism increases in the West, along with a rising belief in aliens – it was only a matter of time before disasters led to people calling these disasters an "Act of Thanos".

When half of the world's population disappeared, Christians were quick to declare it definitely was the rapture, only to then realise that they were the ones left behind with all those ungodly people they'd been pointing the finger at.

The reformed community, in particular, took this news hard. There simply had to be another reason. After all, their theology was spot on.

A thorough investigation of trending topics on Twitter led them all to conclude that the fault lay at the feet of Thanos and his actions in the so-called "Infinity War". Unfortunately, there appears to be no biblical precedent for attributing destruction to a square jawed purple being.

At first, Christians speculated that Thanos was the Behemoth mentioned in Job 40, but none of the Marvel films so far show him feeding on grass like an ox. And so, they quickly moved onto identifying him as one of the beasts mentioned in Revelation 13, exercising its power to wage war against God's holy people.

Needless to say, Christians are unsure and have pre-booked their seats to see the Avengers Endgame film where the remaining Avengers are joined by Hanna-Barbera heroes to finally defeat Thanos.

Early figures suggest that this film is set to beat "God's Not Dead III: We really mean it this time!" as the most popular Christian movie since someone other than PureFlix started making Christian movies.

If Thanos is proven to be the cause of these disappearances, Christian churches will be sure to use him as the ideal candidate to blame for their declining church attendance.

Reporter: **John Spencer**

LOCAL WEATHER

Galilee

Rain together with gale force winds expected this afternoon across the region.

The Met office recommends that no fishermen or travellers cross the Sea today as there's a 99% chance of being capsized and drowned.

If you're travelling with Jesus, expect sunshine and a light south westerly wind. The Met office anticipates absolutely no chance of drowning and a 62% chance of realising that Jesus is the Messiah.

WORSHIP NEWS

Holy Spirit's Blessing Blocked by Worship Leader

Last Sunday, members of New Hope Covenant Church in Wetumpka, Oklahoma were denied the blessing of the Holy Spirit during their second service.

Said lead pastor Rick "Ricky" Henderson, "I preached and preached my heart out, but it was all for nothing. No one was saved, no one's life changed...it was like I was preaching to an empty room."

According to multiple eyewitnesses, the worship leader, Tom "Lefty" Morgan failed to remove his in-ear monitor during the emotional, acapella chorus of the last praise song before Pastor Ricky came onstage. "I don't know what happened, I removed it during the first service. I just forgot!" exclaimed an obviously distraught and shaken Lefty.

The drummer, Jeff "Ace" Byers saw the events unfolding from his customary position at the back of the stage. "Up to that point, Lefty did everything right. He called an audible and sang the bridge a second time before launching into a three-peat of the chorus. After everyone onstage stopped playing their instruments one by one, Lefty was supposed to remove his earpiece just as the third rendition of the chorus started, but Lefty didn't. He just stood there, singing with his earpiece still in, all loud and proud. I couldn't believe it!"

As every modern-day worship leader of a non-denominational church knows, the Holy Spirit is released to bless the rest of the service – including the pastor's sermon and the crowd's response – once the worship leader removes his in-ear monitor. Without said removal, the Holy Spirit is blocked.

For the unfortunate souls at New Hope Covenant's second service, that blessing was tragically missing. "I really felt sorry for visitors," said Pastor Ricky. "Our regular attendees have received blessings in past services, but I'm concerned that visitors might not come back since it was missing this past Sunday."

According to at least one credible source, Lefty has been seen practicing the removal of his earpiece more than 100 times in rehearsal since last week's service in the hopes of avoiding the same mistake.

Reporter: **Jeff the Comma Head**

TECHNOLOGY

Bible App Adds Tools to Limit Time Users Spend on App

This week Facebook and Instagram announced new tools to help users better manage their time online and to set daily limits on their apps.

Realising the negative effects that social media has on young people, the director of research at Facebook, David Ginsberg, said: "Our hope is that these tools give people more control over the time they spend on our platforms."

This is in response to the "Time Well Spent" movement which seeks to fight back against the intrusive effects of technology on our lives.

The Bible App has been the first app to follow the example set by these media giants. It immediately announced tools within its app to limit the Bible's intrusive effects on people's lives.

"It's important in this day and age to ensure that we maintain a healthy balance between the Bible and real life," said a spokesperson, "it's all too easy to spend too much time reading

God's word and not enough time looking at cat memes or seeking validation from others."

Liberals welcomed the decision, "Limiting the time spent reading the Bible will help people adopt a more inclusive and culturally sensitive outlook on life."

Reporter: **John Spencer**

CARTOON

The Camel and the Needle

"I think you missed the point..."

@Furious_Xtian

CELEBRITY NEWS

David Platt to Stop Trying to Convince Christians to Live Biblical Lives

Washington DC – After the success of books such as, "Radical" and "Counter Culture" which challenge Christians to be willing to give up everything and follow Jesus, just as the original disciples did, David Platt is shifting gears.

Reports from his church, McLean Bible Church, are indicating Platt has been asked by his church leadership team to "lighten up a little" and preach sermons that are deemed more appropriate to American culture.

"At first, he seemed a little resistant to the idea," claims a church member who requested to remain anonymous, "But he's come around to a more... 'American' way of thinking."

Platt stated that he intends to even write a new book, with the working title, "You Probably Don't Really Need Jesus After All," slated for a Fall 2019 release.

Platt's next sermon series titled, "Love Your Neighbour, Unless You Don't Like Them," reflects this change in attitude.

Platt's only comment was, "If Joshua Harris can write a book called, 'I Kissed Dating Goodbye,' and then change his position, I see no reason why I can't do the same."

Pastor Platt also requested that people stop saying on Twitter that he looks like a half-starved Tom Brady, as he says that is hurtful.

So, please stop doing that.

Reporter: **Crass Christian**

CHURCH NEWS

Church Divided Over Pumpkin Spice Communion

Autumn (or Fall for our American readers) is here, according to Starbucks. That can only mean one thing. Pumpkin Spice seeks world domination with everything from lattes to breakfast cereals and from hand soap to candles taking up the scent.

Since Pumpkin Spice Season's inception in 2003, it was only a matter of time before the Church was affected by this cultural phenomenon. Communion was the obvious choice.

"Jesus chose to commemorate his sacrifice with foodstuffs that were common in the day, bread and wine. Had he been born today then he would've used doughnuts and pumpkin spiced lattes," stated Prof Dayton of Leap of Faith Theological College.

In response, John MacArthur issued a strongly worded statement against Pumpkin Spice Communion claiming it was the spawn of the consumerist culture that was seeking to infiltrate the holy church. He likened the saccharine flavoured, chemical-laden concoction to the "promise of sin that leaves you only sick afterward."

His statement led to a grassroots campaign "Make Communion Great Again" across the South. It's goal: to ensure that pumpkin spice is removed from all communion wafers.

However, such comments are an anathema to churches that have long had coffee shops as an integral part of their worship. "The church needs to keep with the times," said Pastor Jon of Resting Place Community Church, "You can't expect people to get up in the afternoon to attend church without some caffeinated sugar rush to keep them going. It's the unleavened from heaven. Besides, we're already taking up our cross by getting dressed on a Sunday."

Visionary megachurch leader Jed Obadiah responded, "Pumpkin Spiced Communion is so 2014, the Church should be leading culture, not the other way around."

Despite being only September, his church is already offering Candy Cane flavoured wafers and mulled wine to keep one step ahead of the worldly season.

Reporter: **John Spencer**

BULLETIN

~~Gossip~~ Prayer Requests and Praises

Please continue to donate to Brother Crass' continued medical care. Praise God, He reports the rash has largely subsided and the treatments for the boils have been reduced to three times per week. He is still in need of new undergarments, as most of his are now beyond repair.

Let's celebrate with Brother Smith on his weight loss. He once was a big deal, but now he's half the man he used to be. Join us for cake after the service.

Please remember to pray for little Susie Wilkins's best friend's uncle's co-worker's cat, Jeff. He has a persistent cough that won't go away.

Remember in prayer, Sister Agatha Worker who was injured in the church nursery this week when little Johnny Bratt tried to grab her "special nursery juice." She tore a tendon in her shoulder when picking him up by his shirt collar.

Finally, Sister Ethel has requested prayers for her "friend" who is struggling with something that she doesn't feel comfortable in sharing. But I think we can all guess that it might have something to do with those dubious romance novels she was seen buying at Target. Please share this with the others not here today.

Reporter: **Furious Christian**

THEOLOGY

New Test Determines Accuracy & Relevancy of Scriptures

Exciting theological news from Dallas Divinity School! A test has been developed to help academics and even non-academics determine whether a passage of Scripture is God-breathed and/or applicable to today's culture. It involves answering one simple question:

"Do I agree with this passage?"

If the answer is "yes" then you can be sure that the passage is indeed God-breathed. Whereas if the answer is "no", then the passage is clearly not divinely-inspired but merely the words of man.

The test is also excellent for hermeneutics.

If you agree with a bible passage then clearly it is applicable to today's culture. Whereas if you don't agree, then it's sure to be just a "cultural thing" and thus, it can safely be ignored.

This test is sure to revolutionise the church.

Already topics as diverse as baptism, head coverings, and gifts of the Spirit suddenly are irrelevant/critical* (* delete as appropriate depending on whether you agree or disagree).

Liberal churches are now able to define both Jesus' and Paul's mentions of "sexual immorality" in terms of today's morality rather than those pesky Levitical laws.

Egalitarians are able to ignore all mention of male elders and the word headship as clearly cultural and man-inspired. They are now free to just look at the inspired verses about women in leadership.

"This is wonderful," exclaimed one Christian, "I thought I had to perform a thorough exegesis before I could understand Scripture and its relevance today. But this test means I know straight away what to believe and what to do!"

This test also has the added advantage of removing the need to even spell "hermeneutics" which had been troubling Christians for years.

Reporter: **John Spencer**

LOCAL NEWS

Pastors Bless Planned Parenthood for Supporting Psalm 137

Columbus, Ohio: The Religious Coalition for Reproductive Choice is planning a blessing of the Planned Parenthood abortion centre on the evening of November 9.

The event is called Holy Ground: Blessing the Sacred Space of Decision and is in recognition of the work Planned Parenthood does in fulfilling Psalm 137:9

Blessed shall he be who takes your little ones and dashes them against the rocks!

A spokesperson for the coalition said, "The modern church has unhitched itself from the Old Testament. They limit blessings to the beatitudes and so miss out on all that is available for those who dash infants against rocks. We hope this evening will restore this most ancient and holy practice."

Local worship leader Cindy Lot has composed a song especially for this occasion, "I am honoured to be able to ensure that all of this worshipful Psalm is sung. Too many bands, such as Boney M, just talk about the Rivers of Babylon and miss out the catchy later verses."

The coalition is also planning to release a Prayer of Jabez style book to help people to receive more of this blessing in their lives.

Reporter: **John Spencer**

ARTS & MEDIA

PureFlix Popular Christian Movie Guide Contains Printing Error

We were excited at Northworst Seminary when we heard that PureFlix was coming out with their Most Popular Christian Media Guide. Our faculty is always looking for good clean movies that our students and faculty can watch.

Much of our theology has been shaped by Kirk Cameron and The Left Behind Series. We show A Man called Peter every fall to our new students.

But we've been at a loss lately to find good movies that we can recommend.

That is why we were disappointed when we opened the PureFlix Christian Movie Guide. We purchased one for each of our executive team and decided to comb through it together. However, as we all opened up the guide the pages were blank.

We reached out to PureFlix for an explanation and they told us that the guide was accurate.

Reporter: **Northworst Seminary**

RELATIONSHIPS

Personal ads

Young, loyal and hard-working Moabite recently widowed. Looking for kinsman-redeemer to glean with and a rescue me from a bitter mother-in-law. No upper limit to age.

- **Ruth**

Samaritan woman looking for love in all the wrong places. Five previous husbands let me down and my current man not willing to commit. Looking for something more lasting and hoping you will be my lucky number seven.

- **Anonymous from Sychar, Samaria**

Rich, musical playboy after God's own heart looking for some springtime romance whilst everyone else is away fighting. Single or married – for the right one I'll clear all obstacles, except God.

- **David**

SCIENCE

First Black Hole Image Looks like "Blank Screen"

Yesterday, the first ever image of black hole was revealed in a press conference.

The image was formed from the Event Horizon Telescope (EHT), a network of eight radio telescope spanning locations from Antarctica to Spain and Chile. Taking over two years, and at the cost of more than 50 million USD, this project involved well over 200 mathematicians and scientists.

Sheperd Doeleman, EHT director gushed: "Black holes are the most mysterious objects in the universe. We have seen what we thought was unseeable. We have taken a picture of a black hole!"

The image revealed a supermassive black hole, at the heart of the M87 galaxy, some 55 million light years from Earth.

The audience's reaction to the end result was something less than hoped.

"It's a blank screen!" joked one man from the back.

"Has something gone wrong with the projector?" asked a woman helpfully.

Slightly ruffled, Sheperd added, "This IS the image. Remember that this is a black hole! A region of space from which nothing - not even light - can escape!"

Nervous laughter ensued as Sheperd tried to regain the momentum of the press conference, "This is not just any old black – it is the blackest of black! This has never been seen before today. Our data was collected with meticulous synchronisation and processed by an algorithm which filtered out noise caused by factors such as atmospheric humidity which could have introduced some lightness or even colour."

By this point, the audience grew restless. "I wish someone paid me 50 million to produce a blank screen," whispered someone on the front row.

Sheperd valiantly attempted to close out the press conference on a positive note, "Given our success, we hope to release an image of another black hole that had been recently located in the UK. Our telescopes are currently monitoring Brexit which is on the event horizon of the EU black hole from which no country can seem to escape."

Reporter: **John Spencer**

EDUCATION

Stanford University Introduces VBS Volunteer Trauma Therapy Program

Stanford University announced the launching of a new Graduate Program into its ever-expanding behavioural science department. The new VBS Volunteer Trauma Therapy Program has been greatly needed and long awaited. Course work will begin in the fall semester of 2018.

Ever since the advent of the summer Vacation Bible School (VBS) concept, volunteers have been traumatized by children's behavioural issues such as: inability to remain in one chair for more than 30 seconds, failure to find their "inside voice," running in the sanctuary, and spilling Kool-Aid rather than drinking it. Then there are the food allergies, bladder issues, runny noses, skinned knees and other injuries, misplaced shoes and other clothing items. And what VBS volunteer hasn't had to deal with kids left at church when their parents "lose track of time" and forget to pick up their child? All combined, it takes a toll on those who volunteer after being promised they'd have a lot of fun.

Experts have compared VBS Volunteer Trauma to P.T.S.D. and have created on a program to adequately train therapists in this very specialized area.

Thanks to Stanford University and its new VBS Volunteer Trauma Therapy Program, many victims will finally receive the help they need to recover. Developers of the program realize that the help is only temporary and most suffering from this disorder will relapse come next year's VBS season.

Reporter: **Dr Parson Peeves**

CELEBRITY NEWS

Toby Mac Wins Dove Award for Most Theologically Accurate Song of the Year

Kevin Michael McKeehan, known by virtually no one by this name, is the same guy the CCM world knows as TobyMac.

Although it was no surprise to him, but he acted shocked as his name was announced as the winner of the category for Most Theologically Accurate Song of the Year after quoting a portion of Psalm 23 from the King James Version of the Bible.

While a couple other songs were close to being nominated for mentioning "God" or similar terms for deity, Toby's song was considered by some to be a sermon in itself. Thus, placing it in the ranks of some of the greatest biblical songs of all time, bested only by "Turn! Turn! Turn!" (To Everything There Is a Season, based on Ecclesiastes 3:1-8) by the Byrds.

In his newest radio release "I just need U", TobyMac hints at McKeehan's secret passion to be an evangelist in the event that the 53-year-old vocalist ceases to be hip any longer.

We still do not have any word if professions of faith were made at any of Toby's Hits Deep Tour Live concerts, but we can imagine with that much Bible being presented at 120 decibels, someone is bound to understand what he is saying. In the opinion of the Cee staff, TobyMac is a legend.

Reporter: **Angry Nursery Worker**

DEAR CRASS

Pastor Appreciation Month

Dear Crass,

October is Pastor Appreciation month, and I'm not sure if our church is doing anything for Pastor Tim.

What do I do? How can I motivate the entire congregation to show our pastor how much we appreciate his hard work, his devotion to preaching the Word, the fact he shovels snow at 4am in January so nobody slips on their way to service, and everything else he does for us? I just... we just can't express how much we love this guy by just giving him a mere gift card to Red Lobster, can I... I mean, we?

Please help,

Appreciating in Arkansas

❦

Dear Appreciating,

For starters, make sure you tell your pastor you appreciate him.

Tell him that a lot.

Look deep in his eyes to the point it makes you both feel uncomfortable when you say it to him in person.

Call his house late at night, blocking your number, and when he answers, pause for a few seconds, then whisper huskily, "I appreciate you." before hanging up suddenly.

Find his address in the Church directory and send him several letters a day during the month of October.

I promise you, the more awkward you can make it, the better he will feel.

Please do this, because who wants a pay raise, or bonus check, or free meal for the family?

Make that man feel as though he is loved, adored, and worried that if he ever were to leave, you'd murder his pets.

Yours

Crass

If you would like Crass to give you a condescending and irreverent reply to your heartfelt questions, then email **DearCrass@saltycee.com**.

Get the Cee Delivered Straight to Your Spam Folder!

Don't get enough spam? Or get plenty of it but fancy a bit of variety?

Well look no further.

Sign up to the Salty Cee's mailing list and receive an email every Friday chock full of links to the week's articles. Rest assured that your email provider will classify this link-laden message as spam.

You could instruct it otherwise, but where would the fun be in that?

> http://www.saltycee.com/signup

Subscribers to our mailing list will receive a free e-copy of this book.

Which probably makes you wish you'd signed up before.

Sorry about that.

But I'm sure the chaps at the Cee will come up with some other cool bonus soon.

Think You Can Do Better?

Talk is cheap!

Put your money where your mouth is and send us a submission at:

> www.saltycee.com/submissions

We pride ourselves on being a welcoming community of Christians.

We only ask that it is funny, subtle, and not mean.

We reserve the right to tweak it to meet our requirements or to give you some bad news.

We always credit the author and are happy to promote your work or page in return. However, for legal reasons, your article will become the property of the Salty Cee, so if someone sues they'll only make £1 out of us rather than lots of money out of you. However, if your article is ever included in a future book, then we'll obviously send you a free e-copy or audio version.

Regulars get to join our writers' *Hall of Anonymity* and Twitter message group where we bat around ideas and generally have fun.

Feedback

What an odd word.

How exactly do you feed a back?

I mean it's not like it's got a mouth or anything?

Whilst you're pondering this deep thought, why don't you head on over to Amazon or Goodreads and scribble a short heartfelt review there.

Unless, of course, you want to say how this book wasn't funny. If that's the case, why not continue pondering the word feedback just a while longer until you forget the previous paragraph.

About the Salty Cee Team

Well, we have to admit that we're a little surprised that you're still reading. After all, the "interesting" stuff finished a couple of pages back.

Since you're still here, we might as well share a little about the team of writers on the off-chance that it forms some kind of special bond between us that makes you want to write a really good review.

John Spencer

John was born at a very young age with his umbilical cord wrapped around his neck. At first, it appeared that no lasting damage had been done, but as he grew it became clear that his sense of humour had been damaged irreparably.

When he's not wrestling with work-life balance or literally wrestling with his four children, he's wrestling with writing funny words on a page in his cramped study.

You could buy one of his many other books to make him feel all squiggly inside.

John lives with his family near Oxford, England where daily he wonders how his wife still finds the same jokes funny after more than 20 years of marriage.

Angry Nursery Worker

Angry Nursery Worker got tired of the kids in the pew behind her kicking her seat and decided "If you can't beat 'em, join 'em" (with the emphasis on "beat") and the rest is history made up of grainy police mugshots.

She drives a 1986 Buick Skylark, lives alone (since she forgot where she left her husband on a shopping trip in 1992), and drinks "teething serum" by the pint.

She shares tales of her nursery experiences on Twitter often with the hashtag **#NurseryNightmares**.

Crass Christian

Always lets you know that he's the humblest Christian you'll ever meet.

He recently took a break from Twitter to focus on his prayer life – but before he left he made sure he let everyone know just how holier he was than them for taking a break.

Furious Christian

~~Married male seeking platonic weekend friendship. He enjoys 80s mix tapes, Hallmark movies, and long walks on the beach~~.

Furious is committed to raging about your pet issues on Twitter. He is a worship leader, theology student, and Bible teacher who is much better at making fun of people than loving them.

He lives with his wife and four kids in central IL where he is certain winter will someday steal his will to live.

♖ Dr. Parson Peeves™ ♖

I'm a real parson, with real peeves. I'm not sure why I write anonymously, but I think it has something to do about the mystery of it all or to keep me from getting fired.

Northworst Seminary

Northworst Seminary is your leader in Non-biblical education.

We are a school that excels in judgmentalism and legalism.

Our motto is "We judge so you don't have to."

Dripping Ether
Called upon to save the day every time a parishioner faints from dehydration during a long, dry sermon.

Jeff the Comma head
I may be a nobody with a sense of humour, but at least I'm saved by the Grace of Jesus Christ, who I assume also has a sense of humour...if my life is any indication.

ProtestAnt-Man
Not the actual ant-man.

Peter James
Doesn't write articles based on true events. Honest.

Other books by the Salty Cee Team

Clearly you are keen to still be reading this after all those boring biographies. Sounds like you're the ideal ~~sucker~~ candidate for us to ~~flog~~ mention other books that members of our team have written.

John Spencer

Not the Bible Titles
Different takes on the bible designed to make you laugh and think. Available as ebooks, paperbacks and audiobooks.

Not the Parables of Jesus

More Not the Parables of Jesus

Still More Not the Parables of Jesus

Not the Parable of the Good Samaritan

Not the Christmas story Vol 1
(with devotional)

Christian Parody Titles

Available as ebooks, paperbacks and audiobooks.

Not the Love Dare

Nick Angelis aka Dripping Ether

Christian skits, general silliness and medical satire.

Christian Skits & Such

Nonsense

The Twerk Vaccine

And finally...

Well this is awkward.

We never imagined that you'd even read through our list of books and still keep going. I bet you're one of those people who enter iron man competitions or run marathons for fun.

We're really not quite sure what to do now as we've run out of things to say.

Wait, what in the world could that be over there?

sounds of footsteps fading into the distance while you are distracted

www.ingramcontent.com/pod-product-compliance
Lightning Source LLC
Chambersburg PA
CBHW070953080526
44587CB00015B/2285